MAKING DIFFERENCE WORK

MAKING DIFFERENCE WORK

Copyright © 2018 Courtney Richards

Published by Beyond Expectations Media

ISBN 978-1-912845-08-8 (sc)

ISBN 978-1-912845-09-5 (e)

All rights reserved. No part of this publication may be reproduced, stored in a retrieval system, or be transmitted, in any form, or by any means, mechanical, electronic, photocopying or otherwise without prior written consent of the publisher.

Any people depicted in stock imagery provided by iStockphoto and Unsplash, are models and such images are being used for illustrative purposes only.

All Scripture quotations marked (NKJV) are from the New King James Version of the Bible. Copyright © 1979, 1980, 1982 by Thomas Nelson, Inc. Used by permission. All rights reserved.

All Scripture quotations marked (AMP) are from the Amplified Bible. Old Testament copyright © 1965, 1987 by Zondervan Corporation. The Amplified New Testament copyright © 1954, 1958, 1987 by the Lockman Foundation. Used by permission. All rights reserved.

All Scripture quotations marked (ESV) are from The Holy Bible, English Standard Version. Copyright © 2001 by Crossways Bibles. Used by permission. All rights reserved.

All Scripture quotations marked (NLT) are from the Holy Bible, New Living Translation. Copyright © 1996, 2004. Used by permission of Tyndale House Publishers. All rights reserved.

All Scripture quotations marked (EXB) are from The Expanded Bible, Copyright © 2011 Thomas Nelson Inc. All rights reserved.

Welcome!

Thank you for taking this journey today. I pray your investment of time is richly rewarded as you open your mind to wisdom and revelation truth about your relationships.

This program can eliminate years pain, disappointment and wasted experiences.

Life is always teaching us something. The lessons we learn from the situations of life are entirely based on our individual worldview. Do you live in a friendly or hostile universe? Einstein said the answer to this question is the most important decision you'll ever make.

3 Great Laws

- The Law of Entropy
- The Law of Observation
- The Law of the Seed

These 3 laws when combined together create something quite spectacular.

The Law of Entropy creates the understanding that we've been given delegated dominion & authority (Genesis 1:28) and unless we do something positive, nature (default position of chaos & disorder) will take its course. We have to enforce order. According to Psalm 1:1 (AMP), we are blessed when we choose not to be a passive and inactive bystander in the situations of life.

The way in which we see & perceive things (The Law of Observation) determines our emotions, our expectations and what we ultimately do about situations and circumstances around us; and The Law of the Seed teaches us that we have the ability and power to change our future by what we do with the seed in our possession today. We have the ability to root out bad seeds and plant new ones for a desired harvest.

Understanding and making use of this knowledge with fundamentally transform your relationships.

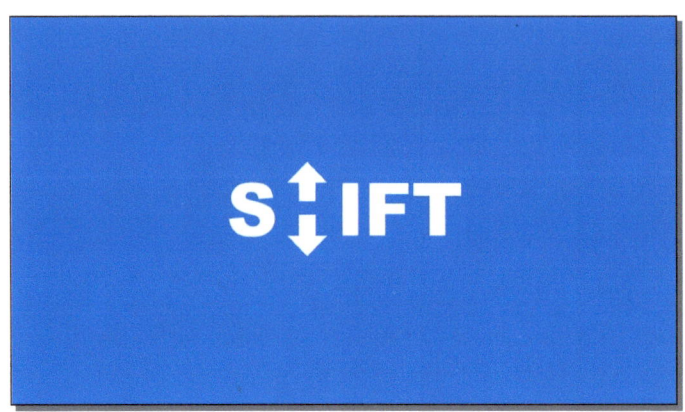

Ready, Steady, **SHIFT**

Please circle the Y = yes or the N = no, in answer to the following questions.

Ready

There is time in my life to invest in my own development	Y or N
A gap exists between where I want to be and where I am right now	Y or N
I can work on tasks that will help me to develop and grow	Y or N

Willing

I am willing to perform whatever is necessary to reach my goal and aims	Y or N
I am willing to SHIFT in my thinking concerning relationships and marriage	Y or N
I am willing to attempt new ways of achieving my goals	Y or N

Able

I have the commitment I need to succeed	Y or N
I have the support I need to make significant changes to my life	Y or N
I am mentally ready for a different approach to my life	Y or N
I am physically prepared for the encounters I may not have experienced before	Y or N

7-10 Y This program will be effective, exciting and rewarding for you

5-7 Y You may need to make some adjustments before starting this program

1-5 Y You are not interested in SHIFTING!

What do you want to get from this program? ....
....

MAKING DIFFERENCE WORK

Use the notes sections in this workbook to make notes whilst the facilitator takes you through the session.

Did you know that there are around 250,000 marriages in Britain each year costing around £2.5Bn

No-one gets married expecting to get divorced (unless it's a business arrangement). However, at a ratio of nearly 1 in 2 and costing around £40,000 per couple, there are around 115,000 divorces every year.

OUR AIM

Relating—and the quality of our relationships—is of deep, natural, and inherent concern for all of us and like any human endeavour, takes attention, care, and commitment. This program is designed to help you create a SHIFT in your thinking that supports the building of strong relationships allowing you to flourish whether single or married.

For those that are already married, it could serve as a means of identifying where things may have gone wrong and a platform for making things better.

You'll discover a possibility of being related independent of your past, your expectations, your preferences, or your views—a dimension more powerful than personality or circumstance—a dimension where relationships can become an occasion for creativity, vitality, intimacy, and self-expression.

Marriage Beyond Expectations:

- We offer specialist programs covering various aspects of improving relationships.
- We also offer Mediation/ Conflict Resolution service & Relationship Coaching
- Get in touch on 07957125137 or hello@marriagebeyondexpectations.com
www.marriagebeyondexpectations.com

Do not be conformed to this world, but be transformed by the renewal of your mind, that by testing you may discern what is the will of God, what is good and acceptable and perfect. Romans 12:2 ESV

Our quest is to wage war on diseased thinking and to embed the divine truth.

As a man thinks so is he... Therefore, your relationships resemble your thinking.

If a member of your team came to you in 1975 and told you they'd invented the digital camera, what would you do? Would you shove them in a cupboard in the hope that the product never reached the mass market? Effectively, that's what Kodak did.

Kodak invented the first digital camera, but when Steve Sasson went to the bosses they refuted the ideas and side-lined the project.
In 1989 the first DSLR camera was launched, yet Kodak refused to make a digital camera themselves on the basis that it would affect the sales of other areas of the photographic business – which they mostly monopolised.
Kodak made billions from the patent – until it ran out in 2007. Five years later in 2012 the company that lasted over 100yrs and was synonymous with photography filed for bankruptcy.
Kodak has disappeared because the senior management refused to listen to their staff and appreciate a different point of view.

About your relationships and specifically marriage, are you getting the best results possible?

Today, our focus is on understanding our individual differences and the needs and wants of your loved ones when they communicate. To move from annoyance to creating an effective, purposeful team.

I want to challenge you to think on things that motivates growth in your relationships.

CHALLENGE: **To make the small changes that'll make a big difference**

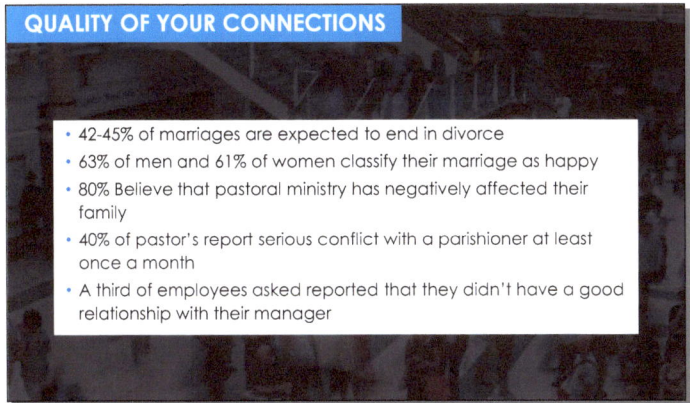

When you start a new job, visit a new church or embark on a marriage – it's all about a relationship, and to each of these relationships there is a maturation process.

CHECKING
At this stage the couple (or group) is still a collection of individuals. Individuals are coming to terms with what behaviours are acceptable as each attempts to manage the transition to being a married unit (or team).

- Participation is sporadic and often hesitant
- Discussions focus on peripheral symptoms or problems rather than central issues
- Sticking to safe ground and are not open about their feelings

CONFLICT
This stage is marked by conflict – hostility and challenging of ideas – interpersonal hostility. The couple (or team) becomes more open, but lacks the capacity to act in a unified, and effective way. Many couples (or teams) fall apart at this stage (checking out of the relationship), but if handled well it can be turned around to a new and more realistic setting of norms & co-operation.

- Disunity, tension and jealousy
- Confusion about boundaries of individual's roles
- Infighting, defensiveness and competition within the team or marriage
- Point-scoring and put-downs
- Polarisation of team members into cliques

CO-OPERATION
This is arrived at when the couple (or team) is ready to move on – when they become frustrated with the atmosphere and lack of progress of

conflict *(pain isn't an enemy, it's merely proof of the existence of one)*. They will endeavour to establish workable rules and practices. This will include how the marriage (or team) should work together.

- Patching up previously conflicting relationships
- Attempt to achieve harmony and manage conflict
- Developing intimacy by sharing personal concerns
- Expressing of own feelings more skilfully and constructively
- Establishing and maintaining team boundaries
- Greater participation and genuine listening
- The development of a cohesive team spirit

CONSTRUCTIVE

At this stage the relationship, the couple (or team) will be capable of diagnosing and resolving both technical and emotional problems. It should be able to make informed decisions about difficult issues. As a result; becomes fruitful, thriving and productive where great things are accomplished - including affecting your children and the wider community.

- Well-developed insight into individual and team needs and behaviours
- Constructive feedback given and received
- Resourceful, creative and effective problem solving
- Differences of opinion seen as constructive, not a personal attack
- Wholehearted commitment to achieving the common goal
- Great confidence in themselves and in how the marriage (or team) operates.

REALITY CHECK

Many marriages never go past stage two, resulting in the following relationship states:
- There are those who stay together and sleep in separate beds
- There are those that stay together but live separate lives
- There are those that stay together but actively wish they were apart

Question to self… Consider your significant relationships and answer:

What stage is my relationship in?

WHAT HAPPENS WHEN THE IMPACT IS NEGATIVE?

- Spiritual & work productivity goes down
- Squabbles occur
- Motivation flat lines
- Trust is visibly diminished
- Doing the minimum at home, work and in ministry

Did you know...

You are 35% more likely to become severely ill, or experience regular illness, if you are in an unhappy marriage. They believe people who are unhappy with their spouse could be at higher risk of depression, high blood pressure and even heart disease.

Researchers found a huge decline in happiness after the first four years of marriage, followed by another decline in years seven to eight. Half of all divorces occur in the first seven years of marriage- hence the term 'seven-year-itch'.

The symptoms displayed by a relationship in a state of disengagement and unhappiness are often characterised by childish behaviours for example: putting on the waterworks, regular bouts of sulking and hostility. None of which is the correct state of mind for building understanding and creating solutions.

Considering the state of your relationship:

- ✓ What will you **START**, **STOP** or **CONTINUE** to move towards the Co-operation and Constructive stages?
- ✓ What changes will you commit to? List them

EXPOSING DISEASED THINKING

Synergy is: Celebrating differences, Teamwork, Open-mindedness, Finding new and better ways

Synergy is not: Tolerating differences, Working independently, Thinking you're always right, Compromise

The most basic meaning of synergy is **when TWO or more people worked together in order to create a solution that is much better than what either person could have done by themselves.**

Like the Apostle Paul saying he was pressing towards the high call... Phil 3:14, synergy is the reward of working together in order to properly achieve a high goal. It works when you think "Win- Win" and when you seek first to understand.

IT IS NOT YOUR WAY OR MY WAY - **IT IS THE HIGHER WAY**

Synergy is	Synergy is not
Celebrating differences	Tolerating differences
Teamwork	Working independently
Open-mindedness	Thinking you're always right
Finding new and better ways	Compromise

Shunners: People that fear differences. They believe their way is the best and the only right way.

Tolerators: They believe that everyone has the right to be different. Their motto is *"don't bother me and I won't bother you"*.

Celebrators: Value difference. They believe that difference sparks creativity and opportunity. They believe differences lead to advantages.

In the knowledge that whatever is celebrated will increase:

In what ways can you recognise and celebrate the difference demonstrated by those you are connected to in all forms of relationships?

Are you SHIFTING?

For example, I thought……. (old beliefs, I now reject), today I'm moving towards (new beliefs)...

List the ways below:

> **REASONS FOR DISENGAGEMENT**
>
> **Myths:**
>
> - We all tend to believe that others see the world as we do
> - We believe that everyone views us the same way we see ourselves
> - Leads to mismatched/ unmet needs

We all tend to believe that others see the world as we do.

We believe that everyone views us the same way we see ourselves.

This leads to mismatched/ unmet needs

Question: Does 1+1=2 all the time? If no, when does 1+1 not equal 2?

What's the impact on my relationships when:
- I don't appreciate my spouse, loved one's or team's point of view?
- I judge them based on my own fixed frame of reference?

As well as being a story about pride - The Tower of Babel project (Genesis 11) failed because of a lack of effective communication.

Two cannot walk together unless they agree Amos 3:3

People don't hear what you're saying they interpret what you say... through our own filters of conditioning we distort, delete or generalise information around us, creating perceptions and reactions based on our own personal reality.

The effectiveness of communication is governed by many factors
- ✓ Age
- ✓ Education
- ✓ Values
- ✓ Past experiences
- ✓ Personality etc.

Giving no room in your mind for other perspectives and ideas will cause inflexibility and leads to judgemental criticism of your spouse, family or co-workers.

Without being appreciated and navigated correctly, these differences all contribute to disengagement in our relationships whether at home, work or further afield.

- ✓ What areas of my relationship is showing signs of poor communication?
- ✓ What can you do to seek understanding?

List what you'll need to **start, stop or continue**.

3 GREAT LAWS

- Law of Seed
- Law of Entropy
- Law of Observation

Creating Order
Order is the correct arrangement of things.

- Everything reproduces after its own kind. Likewise, the current state of your relationship is a result of the seeds you've sown and cultivated in the past.
- Good relationships don't just happen. Failed relationships don't just happen either. Both are the result of choices (intentional or unintentional). God sustains all creation by the word of his power. Likewise, our relationships must be sustained, and order enforced, or they will decline, and ruin will happen naturally.
- How you choose to see yourself, your spouse and loved ones will determine your reality of them and how you'll approach and relate to them. Conversely, it also determines how they respond to you.

AREAS TO SHIFT

1. What will you do to put order into the different form's chaos in your relationships?
2. In what ways will your thinking need to change resulting in new seeds being sown in your relationship?
3. In what ways do you need a fresh perspective on your loved ones?

- In what ways am I **SHIFTING**?
- Remember, change is not change until there's change

PERSONAL PROFILE ASSESSMENT

In each of the following rows of four words place an "X" in front of the word that most often applies to you. Be sure each number is marked as you complete all twenty lines

#				
1	daring	lively	logical	flexible
2	convincing	enduring	calm	happy
3	friendly	easily influenced	strong-willed	self-denying
4	thoughtful	competitive	amusing	agreeable
5	easy going	energetic	bottom-line	perfectionist
6	content	independent	active	perceptive
7	steady	advocate	laid back	certain
8	reserved	detailed	spur of the moment	confident
9	list maker	cheerful	good-natured	straightforward
10	commanding	likeable	affectionate	devoted
11	talker	dominant	loyal	listener
12	quiet	unpredictable	ill-natured	unbending
13	inconsiderate	unsure	hard to please	absent-minded
14	doubtful	wishy-washy	impatient	angered easily
15	idle	isolated	noisy	forward
16	loner	changes easily	bossy	lazy
17	tempermental	aimless	disordered	workaholic
18	overacting	procrastinate	headstrong	suspicious
19	critical	rude	scatterbrained	unconcerned
20	insensitive	moody	unwilling	unsettled

- Answer honestly according to who you are not who you want to be.
- Mark one word each row. Total of 20 words marked.

- **Stay on this page until you have completed all 20 questions**
- **DO NOT TURN TO THE NEXT PAGE UNTIL DIRECTED**

Personality profile adapted from Make a Difference - Dr Larry Little

NOTES

This isn't about labelling people. Humans are far too complicated – far too wonderfully made by my God to label – it is about recognising and **VALUING OUR DIFFERENCE**

PERSONAL PROFILE SCORING

	Much Loved Monkey	Leading Lion	Competent Camel	Tranquil Turtle
1	lively	daring	logical	flexible
2	happy	convincing	enduring	calm
3	friendly	strong-willed	self-denying	easily influenced
4	amusing	competitive	thoughtful	agreeable
5	energetic	bottom-line	perfectionist	easy going
6	active	independent	perceptive	content
7	advocate	certain	steady	laid back
8	spur of the moment	confident	detailed	reserved
9	cheerful	straightforward	list maker	good-natured
10	affectionate	commanding	devoted	likeable
11	talker	dominant	loyal	listener
12	unpredictable	unbending	ill-natured	quiet
13	absent-minded	inconsiderate	hard to please	unsure
14	angered easily	impatient	doubtful	wishy-washy
15	noisy	forward	isolated	idle
16	changes easily	bossy	loner	lazy
17	disordered	workaholic	tempermental	aimless
18	overacting	headstrong	suspicious	procrastinate
19	scatterbrained	rude	critical	unconcerned
20	unsettled	insensitive	moody	unwilling
Totals				

Personality profile adapted from Make a Difference - Dr Larry Little

- Copy numbers from profile to corresponding column on scoring sheet
- Add the columns
- Determine your primary and secondary tendencies.
- Generally, your top 2 scores will define how you respond in various situations

ⓘ Did you score in the double digits for a particular trait? This means you operate out of that trait in most situations.

ⓘ Closed scores- 6-4 6-4 or 5-5 5-5
Listen to descriptions and choose what feels right for you.

However you've scored, the most important thing is not how you scored but how it helps you gain self-awareness of your personality tendencies

Leading Lion (Dominance)

Has the ability to "lead the pack" with great vision. This person is very task driven and will do whatever it takes to accomplish the mission. Being in control is very important to this person. Decisive and goal-oriented, the Lion is confident and likes to be challenged in life and at work. They work well in leadership positions; however, he must learn to delegate and communicate the details of the task to others if they are going to be effective. Patience is not a virtue of the Lion. He is capable of attacking others with rudeness and uncaring dominance.

They also tend to repeat their point over and over again as if to make sure you understood what they mean.

Much Loved Monkey (Influence)

Has the ability to communicate very effectively. This person is a people person. The monkey loves to swing from tree to tree and therefore adopts a very versatile and flexible approach to life, work & ministry environment. Relationships are extremely important as is recognition for a job well done. Life and work must be stimulating, or the Monkey will become bored. People skills, understanding and helping others are real strengths.

The Monkey can be overly sensitive to criticism and has a tendency to "monkey around" and play when consistency and concentration are needed.

Competent Camel (Compliant)

Has the ability to stay focused and complete the task. This person is very detail-oriented. The Camel works well with a prescribed set of standards and has the ability to cross the desert until the task is completed. They work well in a systematic environment and strive hard for accuracy.

Always well prepared, the Camel usually has not only plan A but plan B and C as well. They are "go to" people who are very dependable and loyal. Camels tend to be practical and logical, although they can bring mood swings. Once a camel begins the journey, it is extremely hard for that person to change directions. This often leads to inflexibility in life, work & ministry. Camels can be negative and critical toward others as well as toward themselves.

Tranquil Turtle (Steady)

Has the ability to be steady and secure. This person likes well-defined procedures and expectations. The Turtle brings peace, consistency and follow-through to the work place. They have the ability to bring wisdom and insight to specific situations. They excel in jobs with specific skills and training. Family is extremely important to the Turtle. Therefore, constant change would bring a high level of frustration. The Turtle creeps along at a slow speed and can have a hard time making decisions. The higher stress-level, the slower the Turtle goes.

Motivation and initiative can be real challenges for the Turtle.

Key Points - Leading Lion (Dominant)

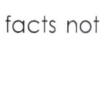

- **Behaviour** – Forceful. Like to take over or assume control.
- **Main motivator** – Power & Authority
- **Biggest fear** – Failure
- **Communication style** – Telling
- **Benefits to relationship** – Getting results. Making decisions. Questioning the status quo.
- **How to relate** – Speak in terms of goals & targets. Give them freedom/ power/ authority. Help them to know their limits
- **How to communicate** – Be clear & specific. Speak about facts not feelings. Don't use too much detail. Don't take too long.

Key Points - Much Loved Monkey (Influence)

- **Behaviour** – Friendly, Influential & People focused
- **Main motivator** – Public praise & recognition
- **Biggest fear** – Rejection
- **Communication style** – Selling/ Encouraging
- **Benefits to relationship** – Motivating others to act. Cultivating relationships & generating enthusiasm
- **How to relate** – Praise & recognise their achievements. Allow them to give their input. Allow them to build relationships
- **How to communicate** – Ask for their opinion. Allow time to build rapport. Be stimulating, fun & fast paced. Don't argue or be impersonal

Key Points - Competent Camel (Compliant)

- **Behaviour** – Logical, systematic & precise. Perfectionist
- **Main motivator** – Standard operating procedures (follow the rules)
- **Biggest fear** – Conflict
- **Communication style** – Writing
- **Benefits to relationship** – Enforcing quality & directives. Improving quality/ standards. Concentration on details & contingency plans
- **How to relate** – Give clear objectives. Provide systems/ rules. Confirm things in writing
- **How to communicate** – Be specific & organised. List advantages & disadvantages. Provide proof. Give things in writing. Don't be confrontational or vague.

Key Points - Tranquil Turtle (Steady)

- **Behaviour** – Good listener. Considerate. Resistant to change
- **Main motivator** – Security
- **Biggest fear** – Insecurity
- **Communication style** – Listening
- **Benefits to relationship** – Completing work thoroughly. Persistent. Developing specialist skills
- **How to relate** – Provide a structured environment. Allow them to finish tasks. Avoid unnecessary pressures/ deadlines. Allow time for change
- **How to communicate** – Listen & ask questions. Show sincere interest. Don't be pushy. Don't force a quick decision.

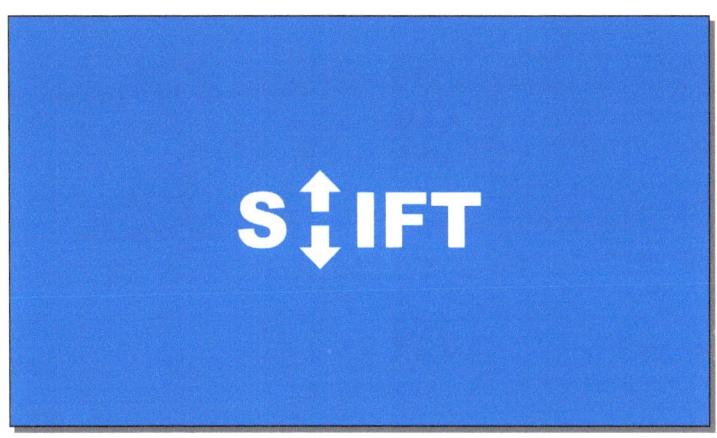

Are you SHIFTING?

For example, I thought....... (old beliefs, I now reject), today I'm moving towards (new beliefs)...

List the ways below:

Behold, You desire truth in the inward parts, and in the hidden part You will make me to know wisdom. Psalm 51:6

In trying to develop self-awareness, please note the following:
Your observable behaviours may mask the real truth, as you may be behaving in a particular way because you may aspire to be that type of person. The downside being acting is tiring - very tiring...

BIGGEST FEAR - Sometimes there is a tendency to mask our true feelings or behaviour tendencies because of fear. Fear will cause us to act and behave in ways that are not beneficial in the long run. For example, a Monkey through fear of rejection may act by rejecting others first or a Lion by fearing failure may procrastinate which ultimately causes them to fail.

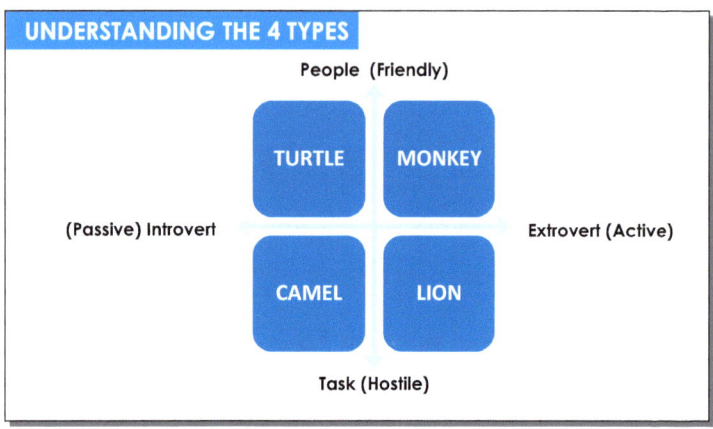

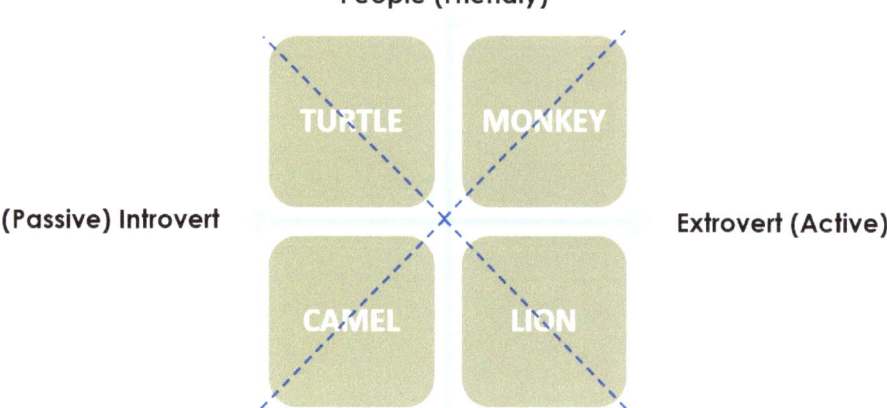

- With zero being the centre, map out your score for each area and place a dot or "X".
- Join your profile points to create a (4 sided) graphic – compare it with your spouse, colleagues or loved ones.
- See how different we are...

- **How you see the world will affect how you respond to challenges**

It's our difference not our sameness that makes great

We all tend to believe that others see the world as we do – **Everyone shares our values,** and we judge them based on our values.

We tend to believe that everyone views us the same way we see ourselves i.e. *"surely everyone sees me the way I see myself"*

JUDGING OTHERS BASED ON OUR OWN FIXED FRAME OF REFERENCE

Lions have a tendency to roar over others that have a different value system – they make quick decisions, big picture – **Task focused extrovert**

They view themselves as strong leaders who gets the job done.

1. Monkeys view them as having few people skills and little regard for others.

2. Camels view them as running over and through the details while missing the quality they find important.

3. Turtles view them as rude, brash & arrogant and not interested in an authentic relationship

Monkeys believe that the most important values are centred around being happy, joyful, verbal – **People focused extrovert**

They view themselves as fun loving. Loving others and making sure everyone loves them

1. Lions view them as being frivolous, unfocused & weak leaders

2. Camels views them as being silly, too playful to be taken seriously. Unreliable & chaotic

3. Turtles views them as too much in your face and fake superficial

Camels value competence & attention to detail. Following the rules and working the plan. Detail, detail... **Task focused introvert**

They view themselves as being dependable, logical, reliable and prepared.

1. Lions view them as too worried about the little stuff & not seeing the big picture
2. Monkeys view them as being boring, up tight & nit-picking
3. Turtles view them as too stressed and anxious, not concerned about people – just processes.

Turtles value humility, working together and a peaceful environment. **People focused introvert**

The Turtle views himself as a peacemaker, as one who has the ability to assess the situation and deliver a wise decision with calmness and steadiness. Also as one with insight and depth.

1. Lions view them as slow, weak and wishy-washy. With impulsive decisions unmet, the lion assumes they have little ability to lead and make swift decisions. Slow decision=no decision.
2. Monkeys view them as someone who is disconnected from others on a surface level. They see them as unapproachable, hard to reach and distant.
3. Camels view them as having a difficult time with follow through and does not pay attention to standards and rules that pertain to decision. They see them as too dependent on relationships and believe they are not able to make logical or rational decisions.

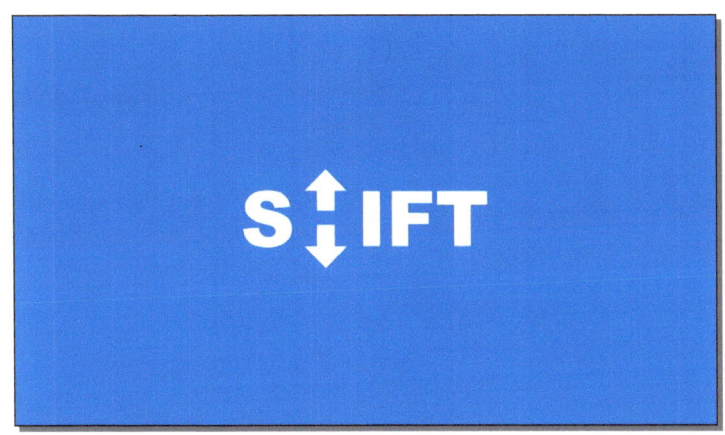

In what ways am I **SHIFTING**?

For example, I thought……. (old beliefs, I now reject), today I'm moving towards (new beliefs)…

List the ways below:

Are you helping those connected to you achieve God's plan for their lives or are you trying to get them to fulfil your own agenda?

Communication is an ongoing and continuously changing process of exchange involving a sender and receiver that reciprocate information (this is effective when there is common understanding).

WHAT'S IN IT FOR ME?
To every action there is a cost and benefit.
All behaviour is costly in that it requires the expenditure of energy and pre-empts time that might otherwise produce other rewards.
What do you hope to get from your expenditure of energy in your relationship?

The standards that people use to evaluate rewards and costs differ from person to person - this contrast in the evaluation of rewards and costs may be attributed to cultural, religious, or personality differences between individuals. Greater rewards are achieved when we choose to develop value and engagement by finding out what's important to our spouse, loved one's (or team members) - this is about understanding the conditions that generate their best.

Every relationship involves an exchange
We tend to avoid relationships, interactions, and feeling states that are dissatisfying or costly and seek out situations and experiences that are gratifying, pleasurable, or rewarding.
In our world of instant gratification, this is a problem as we often fail to see things based on a long-sighted view.

The benefits for working at it, certainly outweighs the benefit of things staying as they currently are - not to mention pleasing God.

HONOUR OR DISHONOUR?

Submitting yourselves one to another in the fear of God. Eph 5:21

- What can do to validate or invalidate those we love or lead?

- What is servant leadership?

How to honour your loved one's…

Each one of us is different and it is important to learn how to validate your spouse and other with which you are in significant relationships. Without realising, you could be unconsciously invalidating them - leading to hurt feelings and disengagement.

How to validate:
- A Lion? By accomplishing tasks – empowerment – they respect strength
- A Monkey? By approval and affirmation (look – touch – words)
- A Camel? Quality of the task specifics – their trigger word is specific
- A Turtle? 121 relationships – trigger word is TIME

Learn to serve each other – help each other get what they want, and you'll always get what you want. Eph 6:8

Submitting yourselves one to another in the fear of God. Eph 5:21

What is your reaction to others different to you? Luke 9:49-55

What will you commit to doing differently?

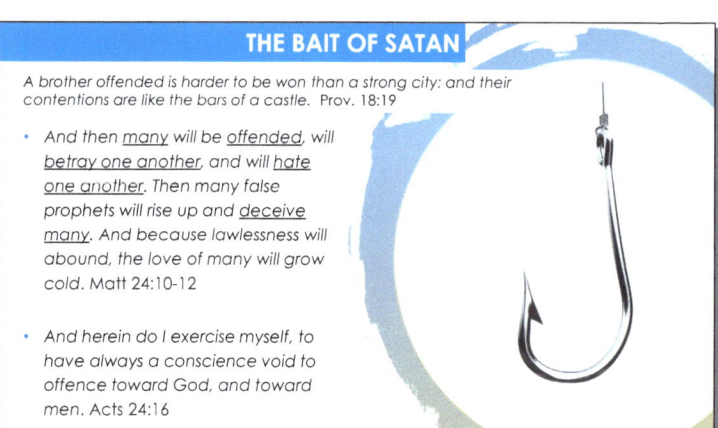

Forgiveness is another aspect of love (decision based giving). Especially when the Word tells us that we all stumble and sin in many ways - forgiveness is something that we all had better learn to get good at - and that includes you!

Holding onto unforgiveness is like drinking poison and hoping that the other person dies... As you are one flesh with your spouse, unforgiveness poisons the entire relationship.

With that said, **can you afford to not give this precious gift?**
God doesn't ask you to give something that you don't already have. He gave you forgiveness by sending his son to die in your place and, therefore expects you to do the same – **especially to your spouse.**

While we're on the subject... the word *offended* in Matthew 24:10-12 is the Greek word *skándalon* – meaning, the trigger of a trap (the mechanism closing a trap down on the unsuspecting victim); (figuratively) an *offense*, putting a *negative cause-and-effect relationship* into motion.
Also, ("the means of stumbling") stresses the *method* (*means*) of *entrapment*, i.e. how someone is caught by *their own devices* (like their personal bias, carnal thinking).
Unforgiveness is therefore a personal trap waiting to hook you.

Are you offended?
Let it go - release yourself.

THE GREAT NEUTRALISER

Exercise...
- Write a list of the people that have done you wrong - think about it, then answer these questions about forgiving them.

- could you?
- would you?
- when?

EXERCISE

While we're not dealing with deep character flaws, specifically, list the offences and vexations you have against your spouse or loved ones based on their difference.

- could you let it go?
- would you let it go?
- when?

Forgiveness is like erasing a debt. *We can't forgive people at dinner and then serve them their wrong deeds at breakfast.*

- Prayerfully seek the heart of God and trust him
- To truly forgive is to allow the other person to forget...
- Maybe you need to forgive you

LIONS
We'd better have lions in our lives and on our team.
We'd better know how to support those lions. They are incredibly gifted people.
Lions fly at 30000 feet. They are big task people.
Lions can go after it, and get it done. They are valuable. We've got to have those people that fly at that level.

MONKEYS
We'd better have a monkey in our lives and on our team. Monkeys understand people. They are our thermometer of people.
Consider this:
What if we remove the people from our home, business or ministry. What would be left? Nothing would be left.
Monkeys have the ability to sense what is happening. (We need that in a team – someone who knows what's happening with morale, who knows if people are loyal, if they buy into the current vision).
We need that empathetic person walking with us, the one who knows our heart. We need the monkey for bringing much needed humour - such great medicine for dealing with difficult situations.

CAMELS
We'd better have a camel in our lives and on our team. Camels are the go-to person on our team. We need Camels.
Camels are the ones who bring the logic and the quality.
They really care about how the job is done. They are the execution experts in terms of process.
They will take us from point A to point B to point C and will walk us through and save us time, energy and money if we will let them help us with those details.

TURTLES

We'd better have a turtle in our lives and on our team. Turtles have the kind of wisdom that when they speak, we'd better listen.

Turtles don't use many words, but the words they do use are powerful. We need to know that and understand that they bring wisdom. They will not force themselves on the group, but if you slow down and give them a chance you will hearing something like this:

I wonder if we...
Have you ever thought about...
What if we...

Turtles phrase things in non-offensive ways. That is so helpful.
Turtles save you time and money; they will make you money.

Why I need you...

List the attributes your spouse or loved one's bring to your life:

VALIDATING THOSE WE LOVE

"The secret to success is valuing diversity within our relationships. We must learn to get the best out of each other, no matter what."

T he secret to success is diversity within our relationships. We must learn to get the best out of each other, no matter what.

My people are destroyed for lack of knowledge Hosea 4:6
There are diversities of gifts, but the same Spirit. There are differences of ministries, but the same Lord. And there are diversities of activities, but it is the same God who works all in all 1 Cor. 12:4-6

As iron sharpens iron, so a man sharpens the countenance of his friend. Proverbs 27:17
The resulting friction and heat causes increase and enhancement - but we first have to overcome the discomfort.

The discomfort caused by difference is designed for our increase. Developing the quality of discipline helps us to see the big picture we are trying to achieve in our relationships. This helps us go through the difficult and uncomfortable patches of a relationship to attain the prize. Like eating greens or liver, we have to learn to do what's good above what is pleasurable.

What steps will you take to make a meaningful difference?

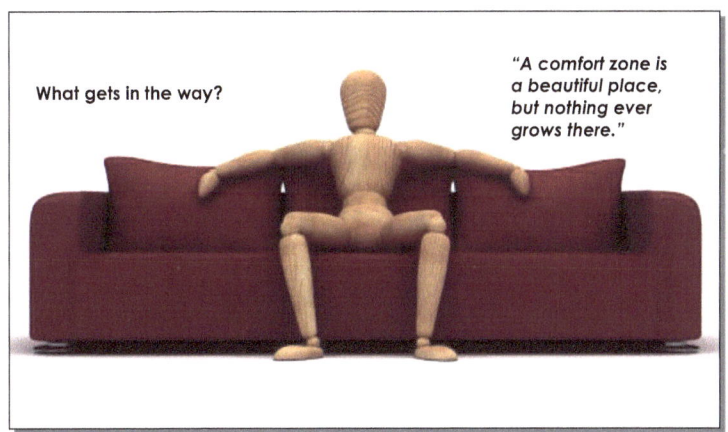

What gets in the way of you coming out of your comfort zone?

- It's not your way of doing things
- It feels counter intuitive
- It's risky

Changing habitual behaviours isn't easy, but it's worth it! We may want to change but the transition to a new normal is what often makes it prohibitive as we often revert back to what we know and are comfortable with.

Consider this example:

You are high Compliance (Camel) individual that like rules and processes and are now in a marriage or other committed relationship with an individual that's high Influence (Monkey) that loves to talk and be with people. Working on validating these different behaviour preferences means the Camel would have to learn to be more Monkey (and vice versa). Coming out of your comfort zone requires more energy when compared doing things as you've always done.

Managing your energy

- Getting out of your comfort zone will, after an extended period of time become draining (loss of energy), so you'll need to recharge your natural energy.
- As a predominant Lion, you will never be a predominant Turtle so don't try – that's where they excel. However, recognise that there are times when you'll need to leave your comfort zone.
- However, renewing your energy is a must by going back to your favoured position thereafter.

KEY MESSAGES

- **Get Uncomfortable** - get out of your comfort zone and be who you need to be.

- **Take Risks** - risk making mistakes, risk growing from our experiences.

- **Reach out to others** - focus on empowering others to develop their strengths

- **It takes work!**

All personalities can make a difference and achieve excellence in relationships. It's not the personality type that determines excellence it's our willingness to:

Get Uncomfortable - get out of our comfort zone and be who we need to be in context with the realities of our environment.
Take Risks - risk making mistakes, risk being vulnerable and growing from the experiences.
Reach out to others - focus on empowering others to develop their strengths

For though I am free from all men, I have made myself a servant to all, that I might win the more; and to the Jews I became as a Jew, that I might win Jews; to those who are under the law, as under the law, that I might win those who are under the law; to those who are without law, as without law (not being without law toward God, but under law toward Christ), that I might win those who are without law; to the weak I became as weak, that I might win the weak. I have become all things to all men, that I might by all means save some. Now this I do for the gospel's sake, that I may be partaker of it with you. 1 Cor 9:19-23

The responsibility of the communication is on the sender not the recipient

> Own your own happiness
> Challenge your story
> Enjoy the journey not the destination
> Make your relationship count
> Work to make things better

What questions do I have?

NOTES

Also available from Beyond Expectations Media

Thinking Fit for Marriage

Built to Last

Chaos To Order

Through The Storm

Untying Fear Knots

Eye 2 Eye

     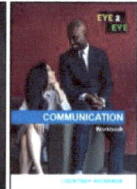

GYMNASIUM
OF THE MIND